PowerKids Readers:

MY SCHOOL™

Meet the
School Secretary

Elizabeth Vogel

The Rosen Publishing Group's
PowerKids Press™
New York

1

Published in 2002 by The Rosen Publishing Group, Inc.
29 East 21st Street, New York, NY 10010

First Edition

Book Design: Michael Donnellan

Photo Credits: All photos by Cindy Reiman.

We extend a special thank-you to Darlene Davis and the S.F.B. Morse Young Child Magnet School in Poughkeepsie, New York for their participation in this project.

Vogel, Elizabeth.
Meet the school secretary / Elizabeth Vogel.
     p. cm. — (My school)
Includes bibliographical references and index.
ISBN 0-8239-6036-6 (lib. bdg.)
1. School secretaries—Juvenile literature.
 [1. School secretaries. 2. Secretaries. 3. Occupations.] I. Title.
LB2844.4 .V64 2002
651'.9371—dc21

                                                      2001000953

Manufactured in the United States of America

Contents

78.657

I am the school secretary.

5

You can find me in the school office or outside the principal's office.

I make the announcements over a loudspeaker each morning and throughout the day. The whole school can hear me!

I collect the attendance from all the teachers. The teachers send a student to give me the attendance sheet. I know who is in school and who is out sick.

11

I hand out the mail to the teachers. I make sure they know about important meetings.

If a teacher is sick and stays at home, I call for a substitute teacher. A substitute is someone who comes in to help teach while the teacher is out sick.

I collect all forms and permission slips for field trips. Sometimes students visit places like museums, farms, or zoos.

I let you know when you can see the principal. The principal is very busy!

Mrs. Darlene
Davis

Principal

19

I help the principal make sure the school runs smoothly. We work together to make sure you are happy and safe at school.

Words to Know

attendance

mail

permission
slips

Here is another book to read about school secretaries:

What School Secretaries Do When No One Is Looking
By Jim Grant and Iry Richardson
Staff Development for Educators

To learn more about school secretaries, check out this Web site:

http://stats.bls.gov/k12/html/red_004.htm

Index

Word Count: 171

Note to Librarians, Teachers, and Parents

PowerKids Readers are specially designed to help emergent and beginning readers build their skills in reading for information. Simple vocabulary and concepts are paired with stunning, detailed images from the natural world around them. Readers will respond to written language by linking meaning with their own everyday experiences and observations. Sentences are short and simple, employing a basic vocabulary of sight words, as well as new words that describe objects or processes that take place in the natural world. Large type, clean design, and photographs corresponding directly to the text all help children to decipher meaning. Features such as a contents page, picture glossary, and index help children get the most out of PowerKids Readers. They also introduce children to the basic elements of a book, which they will encounter in their future reading experiences. Lists of related books and Web sites encourage kids to explore other sources and to continue the process of learning.